Big Fish Results

How to Use the 'Net' for a Bigger Catch

For more information on using the Internet to get more customers, please call Tony Guarnaccia at 401-484-8736 or visit **BigFishResults.com**.

Big Fish Results
How to Use the 'Net' for a Bigger Catch

Copyright © 2013 by Big Fish Results

All rights reserved. No part of this book may be reproduced or transmitted in any form or by any means, electronic or mechanical, including photocopying, recording or by any information storage and retrieval system, without written permission from the author, except for the inclusion of brief quotations in a review.

Library of Congress Cataloging-in-Publication Data
Guarnaccia, Tony
    Big Fish Results
    How to Use the 'Net' for a Bigger Catch

    p. cm.
    ISBN 1492111619

    1. Business & Economics / Marketing / General

First Paperback Edition

Table Of Contents

Big Fish Results

How to Use the 'Net' for a Bigger Catch

Online Marketing for Local Business Introduction 1
    Traditional Marketing Doesn't Work Anymore 1
    Specific Marketing Strategies 2
    Changes in Business 3
    The Potential for Exponential Profit Growth 4
    Statistics You Need to Know 5
    Making Changes to Your Online Marketing Methods 5

Five Things No One Is Doing 7

Online Local Domination 9
    4-Point Online Domination 10

Your Simple Online Marketing Plan 15

Prior to Putting Your Online Marketing Plan in Place 17
    Analyze Your Overall Online Marketing Plan 17
    Analyze Your Online Marketing Plan for Each Line 18

Where to Start 21
Doing Detailed Keyword Research 21
Do Onsite Search Engine Optimization Updates..24
Add a Lead Capture System to Your Website 27
Making Personal Branding Changes 29

Tasks That Repeat 31
Article Marketing...32
Press Releases 35
Video Marketing 37
Mobile Marketing 38
Pay-per-click Campaigns 43
Report Generation, Testing and Tracking 46
Directory Submission 50
Adding Testimonials Creates Validity and More 52
The Importance of Web 2.0..53
Social Media and Social Networking 54
Additional Traffic Strategies..56

Keeping on Top of Things 61
Outsourcing: The Answer to Easy Implementation..62
Choosing the Right Subcontractor 67

Online Marketing for Local Business Conclusion 69
Techniques to Increase Your Business's Profits 69

Online Marketing for Local Business Introduction

If you are the owner of a local business, you are probably suffering from a drop in demand for your products or services as a result of the economic recession most areas have been suffering from for the past few years. In fact statistics show that small local businesses are making 30% to 50% less than they were just a few years ago. Some of the businesses that comprise this statistic include:

- Plumbers
- Dentists
- Locksmiths
- Restaurants
- Plastic Surgeons
- Accountants
- Carpet Cleaners
- Contractors
- Landscapers

Traditional Marketing Doesn't Work Anymore

The fact of the matter is the marketing techniques that were solid and reliable for local businesses to use to reach their market in the past are no longer working. This means *Yellow Pages* ads, newspapers and other types of hard copy advertising are simply not bringing in business. That's because people simply don't use them anymore.

Businesses that are still using such outdated forms of advertising are throwing away thousands and thousands of dollars on ineffective marketing every month. If you are one of those people still investing in such ads, ask 10 people where their copy of the *Yellow Pages* is. Most can't tell you or will tell you they put it in the recycling bin shortly after it arrived. What does that tell you about the money you're spending?

Consumers are looking more and more to the Internet to find information about the services and products they are seeking, even locally. Therefore, if businesses want to reach new customers they simply must have a quality Internet presence. And that does not mean just a lame website that a kid could have put together!

Today's most effective websites are well thought out, interesting, personable and informative. They utilize a variety of savvy online marketing techniques in order to stand out from their competitors. If you have a site with no keywords in it and almost no backlinks, you are missing the boat and will never get to the top of the search engine results.

Specific Marketing Strategies

There are specific marketing strategies that apply uniquely to Internet marketing. If you're not staying on top of these Internet marketing strategies and implementing them, your website will not get traffic and you'll miss out on one of the most efficient, lucrative sources of new customers for your business.

One of the stumbling blocks keeping most local business owners from using online marketing strategies to grow their customer base is that they simply have no idea what needs to be done. Online marketing is so new and such unfamiliar territory for most business owners that they don't know where to start. They spend so much time running their business, taking care of their customers and managing their staff that they don't have the time to learn something new — especially something that's constantly evolving.

Ask yourself a few questions:

- What are long-tail keywords?
- What is keyword density?
- What is Web 2.0?
- How do you set up an autoresponder?
- How do you change the tags on your website?
- How do you create videos and audios for your website?

If you are like most business owners, you can't answer these questions with much certainty. That is absolutely normal. You've wisely spent your time focusing on other aspects of your business — the ones that were crucial for you to master. But now you need to learn more! Finally, the time has come for average local business owners to discover exactly what needs to be done in order to effectively put an online marketing plan in place for their businesses.

Changes in Business

Today, most local business owners are running lean and hungry. They need more work. They need to get more customers in through the door. They need to adapt to the changing economy. Today's business environment is in constant flux — specifically, the whole process of reaching your target market cost-effectively is nothing like it was even a decade ago. Understanding these changes and meeting the challenges they present is essential to the survival of your business.

Case in point: One local business was spending $8000 per month on *Yellow Pages* advertising that cost more than it was bringing in. It doesn't take long before smart business people recognize this as fighting a losing battle, a big problem that needs to be fixed. So they stopped the ad. However, now they have an $8000 budget for marketing but don't know what to do to get the best possible return on their marketing investment.

Because they don't know Internet marketing, they could easily pour those funds into online strategies that either fall flat or backfire. The learning curve is sharp and unforgiving.

But these entrepreneurs realize the Internet is the future. More than 1 billion local searches are performed online every month. This number grows by more than 50% each year. In fact, 80% of people search online before they make a purchase. Even more important, the vast majority of searchers look online for local services and products before they make a buying decision. They now prefer this type of search over *Yellow Pages* or the newspaper. Therefore, business owners need to be online in an effective way.

The Potential for Exponential Profit Growth

Using Internet marketing can easily result in an increase in sales of tens of thousands of dollars. This is amazing considering the sheer number of layoffs, crises, and more that people are facing. The old ways of getting business in the door are broken and they have to learn something new. Many people who thought they had retired find themselves just a couple of years later back working hard in business. They are the people who can use an Internet marketing plan to save their business and their livelihood.

By putting online marketing strategies to work, you are not only positively impacting your own business, you are improving your local economy. More money is being spent locally. With a steady stream of new customers flowing into your sales funnel, downsizing and layoffs become a thing of the past. In fact, your business will grow, despite the economy because you are reaching those who are looking to buy from businesses like yours. And that is what effective marketing is all about!

Online marketing has the potential for exponential profit growth. If you are not ready for your business to double or even more, stop reading now!

Statistics You Need to Know

The following statistics give you a glimpse of how people are using the Internet to find the products and services they need:

- 64% of U.S. Gross Domestic Product comes from local businesses.
- 4.2 million local small businesses have sales in the $500,000 to $20,000,000 range.
- Over 1 billion local searches are performed monthly — a number that grows more than 50% each year.
- 98% of searchers choose a business that is on page 1 of the results they get.
- 41% of clicks go to the #1 ranked site in a search.
- 12% of clicks go to the #2 ranked site in a search.
- 8.5% of clicks go to the #3 ranked site in a search.

These statistics show how important it is for your business to develop and implement an online marketing strategy to get your business to the top of the search engine results so when prospective customers go searching for you (without knowing your name or business name) they find you.

Making Changes to Your Online Marketing Methods

Like most businesses, you probably need to make some pretty drastic changes to your marketing plans to maximize the results you get from online marketing. Here are some insider facts you need to know about marketing your business online:

- The potential to grow your business using online marketing is phenomenal, no matter what industry you are in. You just need to cultivate the opportunity.

- There are five extremely useful Internet marketing techniques that no one is doing. Learn them and put them into practice and you will outperform all your competitors quickly.

- You need to achieve local online domination, a goal you can reach by learning and mastering a four step process. Following these steps correctly virtually guarantees you'll get the results you want.

- Creating and following a proven online marketing plan is essential for managing all the crucial tasks needed to get to the top of the search results and get more new customers into your business.

- Establishing a baseline is critical before you implement a new marketing plan. Take the time to thoroughly analyze what you are already doing and what you need to change so you can measure your progress.

- Make your tasks more reasonable by breaking them down. Start with the tasks that are one-time jobs, as they provide the foundation for your marketing plan, and you will have the pleasure of checking things off your list.

- Only when the one-time tasks are completed should you begin the tasks that repeat. These are long-term commitments that will require monthly, weekly or even daily attention.

- You should consider seeking out subcontractors for a portion of or the entire online marketing plan, for the sake of expediency and skill. There are many who can take on select tasks to facilitate the process for you.

- Create a system for tracking the results from implementing your marketing plan. Measure the increase in your business income.

Five Things No One Is Doing

While some people are using select Internet marketing techniques to drive traffic to their site, others are doing nothing at all, except hoping for the best. Using a wide variety of tried and true online marketing methods is the best way to see real results in your sales. A great place to start is by opting to implement the five things practically no one is doing. These things produce serious results and should be used by every business with an Internet presence. They include:

- Blogging
- Autoresponders, building an email list and following up
- Free reports
- Online video
- Basic SEO

▲ **Blogging**
This creates a steady online presence which increases your chances of being at the top of search engine results for your keywords. Using a blog you can get content containing all your long-tail keywords on the web. In addition, it allows you to build a following of customers and potential customers who are interested in what you share and who provide valuable feedback to you. This audience is ripe for being marketed to when your business is in a slump.

▲ **Autoresponders**
These are tools that allow you to build an email list and easily follow up with those on it. They are a set of standardized letters that are set up once and the necessary contact with each new individual who opts into your email list is taken care of automatically. An autoresponders is an indispensable tool which saves time for you and actually does some of the lead nurturing that is absolutely essential in demand marketing.

▲ Offering Free Reports

Providing these reports to those who are interested is another of the underused tools in the online marketer's toolbox. Everyone loves getting something for nothing. If you offer free reports on an area of interest to your potential customers you will establish yourself as an expert in that field and you will easily be able to get them to give their email or other contact information in exchange for a report that actually provides useful information.

▲ Online Video

This is the video version of blogs and articles. You can reach numerous customers and potential customers with this new hot online marketing tool. You can create a simple video from text slides and voiceover or music or you can record a video of actual products and services in use. Be sure to place video both on your site and offsite for maximum effectiveness.

▲ Basic SEO, or Search Engine Optimization

This is another tool that goes unused by those looking to promote their business online. It is simply making sure that your website is as appealing as possible to the spiders that crawl the Internet collecting information for search engines. This includes strategic use of keywords, backlinks and more.

Many businesses pay a lot of money to have someone create a fancy looking website for them, but it simply is not search engine optimized, so it will never get ranked in the search engine results. Without the strategic use of keywords, a significant number of links to their site and the removal of sluggish elements like Flash, a website will never achieve a top ranking.

By putting in place these five things that no one is doing you will be able to easily set your website apart from that of most of your competitors. Your search engine rankings will begin to quickly climb and you will find that more and more customers are "stumbling across" your website.

Online Local Domination

While it sounds rather ominous, online local domination is exactly what you want for your business in order to be a huge success. Online local domination means that you are the number one authority online for your local market. You get that distinction by taking your business from hard-to-find online to literally being everywhere online. You will be in the top 10 of the local search, natural search and pay-per-click (PPC) campaigns. Your content will show up in top results and you will have more consumer reviews than any other local business in your market.

Once your business is consistently the most popular one found in any type of online search, and you are absolutely everywhere your local customers look, potential new customers quickly come to recognize that you are the authority in your field. They will want to do business with you because they will recognize you as the best. And who doesn't want to do business with the best?

Online local domination is simply being the most readily found business of its type in a given local area. If your business is consistently at the top of local search results, normal search results and geo-targeted generic results, you have achieved online local domination. If your business is at the top of normal search results not including an indicator of area, it is even better.

You can make yourself the master of local results by understanding how searches work. You need to understand the different keywords that are used as individuals search for businesses of your type. This will help you employ different online marketing techniques to help you effectively get to the top of the search engine results, exactly where you want to be.

Page 1 results are what you need and ultimately what matter most because 98% of people searching choose from those page 1 results, no matter what search engine they use. In fact, you want to be in the top three results for your keywords in order to get potential customers to your site. If you are not in those results, you are losing out on a lot of business.

Professional online marketers can get most businesses to number one in the search results for local keywords on Google within one week. This is because most local keywords have very little competition and are therefore ripe for someone with knowledge to come around.

4-Point Online Domination

Start the 4-point online domination process today in order to achieve online local domination. You can be everywhere you want to be online by using:

- Local business results (Google + Local Pages)
- Natural search results
- PPC results
- Content results

Google burger Atlanta

Search   About 26,500,000 results (0.27 seconds)

Web
Images
Maps
Videos
News
Shopping
More

Change location
Show search tools

YEAH! BURGER | Atlanta, GA | Burgers, dogs, salads, ice cream ...
www.yeahburger.com/
Zagat: 22 / 30 - 178 Google reviews

Flip burger boutique
www.flipburgerboutique.com/
Zagat: 23 / 30 - 385 Google reviews
Menu - Atlanta, Buckhead - Atlanta, West Midtown

Grindhouse Killer Burgers
www.grindhouseburgers.com/
Zagat: 23 / 30 - 82 Google reviews

Farm Burger
www.farmburger.net/
Zagat: 24 / 30 - 13 Google reviews

Vortex Bar & Grill
www.thevortexbarandgrill.com/
Zagat: 24 / 30 - 396 Google reviews

Holeman & Finch Public House
www.holeman-finch.com/
Zagat: 27 / 30 - 178 Google reviews

More results near **Atlanta, GA** »

A) 1168 Howell Mill Road
Atlanta
(404) 496-4393

B) 1587 Howell Mill Road
Northwest
Atlanta
(404) 352-3547

C) 209 Edgewood Avenue
Southeast
Atlanta
(404) 522-3444

D) 3365 Piedmont Road
Northeast
Atlanta
(404) 816-0603

E) 438 Moreland Avenue
Northeast
Atlanta
(404) 688-1828

F) 2277 Peachtree Road
NE
Atlanta
(404) 948-1175

Map for **burger Atlanta**

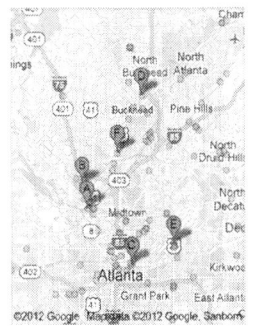

Ads

Google Offers: Pizza K
$15 for $30 worth of food
90% off

See your ad here »

News for burger Atlanta

Best place to get **Atlanta's** original double decker **burger**
Creative Loafing Atlanta - 18 hours ago
The local fast-food institution Zesto has been around since 1949, serving **burgers**, onion rings, chili dogs, milk shakes, and more greasy comfort faves than you ...

Atlanta Burger Joints | Urbanspoon
www.urbanspoon.com/f/9/809/Atlanta/Burger-Joints
Atlanta Burger Joints. Reviews from critics, food blogs and fellow diners.

Atlanta: Top 10 Burgers - Restaurants - BlackBook
www.blackbookmag.com/restaurants/atlanta-top-10-burgers-1.27341
Jan 27, 2009 – Despite the fast food stigma, a slab of cow between two buns has become nothing less than an art form. The following use a red meat palate to ...

Yeah! Burger - Westside / Home Park - Atlanta, GA
www.yelp.com › Restaurants › Burgers
★★★★ Rating: 3.5 - 369 reviews - Price range: $$
369 Reviews of Yeah! **Burger** "I wish I was closer so I could eat here more regularly! I usually go with a beef or bison **burger** topped with cheese, lettuce and ...

Battle of the Burgers - September 8, 2012
www.battleoftheburgers.com/
The 3rd Annual Battle of the **Burgers** - Benefiting Embraced - Saturday September 8. Buy Tickets Now!

Best - Top 10 Burgers in Atlanta Blue Ribbon Grill Gayot
www.gayot.com/restaurants/best-atlanta-ga-top10-burgers_7at.html
Hungry? Come here for the top 10 **burger** joints in **Atlanta**, courtesy of Gayot.com.

Burger 21 Signs Franchise Deal for Two Locations in Atlanta and ...
www.burger21.com/.../burger-21-signs-franchise-deal-for-two-locati...
Jun 7, 2012 – "With consumer demand for fast casual experiences on the rise, we are confident that **Burger** 21 will be a perfect match for **Atlanta** residents ...

Big Fish Results

Local Search Results – Google + Local Pages

One of the components of online domination is being prominent among the local business results in Google + Local Pages. Google + Local Pages is an interactive way for people to find local businesses and, best of all, it is an opportunity for a local business to be featured on page one of Google.

Google + Local Pages, which replaced Google Places, is an important tool for businesses to know and understand so they can use it successfully to market and grow their business online. Google + Local Pages can help businesses rank higher in organic search results, but maybe more importantly, Google + Local Pages can help a business rank higher in local search results.

Google + Local Pages works in connection with Google's social media platform Google +. In fact, every Google + profile has a tool bar to the left of the home page that has a button labeled "local." This button is simply another way for others to find a local business. So, any business that has taken the initiative to register with Google + Local Pages will have the opportunity to see their business prominently displayed when this button is used. Having a local business found in this manner is in addition to being able to be found via mobile apps or through an online search at Google.com or Google Maps.

Google ranks Google + Local Pages results on three factors:

- **Relevance:** If someone searches for a dry cleaner in Houston, then only dry cleaners will show up vs. other types of businesses in the area.

- **Distance:** Google will provide search results based on the general location entered by a searcher or based on the distance between the location of a searcher and a local business.

- **Prominence:** How well-known is the business? Google uses resources throughout the web and provides search results based on how well-known that business is.

Google + Local Pages prominence can be enhanced with plenty of positive reviews left by those using a local business' services. The star rating system Google used was changed after they acquired Zagat and now anyone with a Google + account can write a review based on a 30-point Zagat scoring system. This in turn helps Google rate a local business. Therefore, the better the business' Zagat ratings, the better the business' rank on Google.

The key to making the most of a Google + Local Pages listing is to complete the business profile entirely, accurately, and consistently. Customer reviews are a vital part of creating a complete profile on Google + Local Pages and the more interactive you are with Google + the more you can expect positive reviews, at least by those in your circles.

Natural Search Results

The natural search results are those organic results that are generated by search engine searches and are listed directly below the sponsored ads and the local search results. In addition to your actual website, other things can appear in the natural search results. For this reason you need to pay attention to the use of keywords in the following, because they are all commonly found ranked in natural search results:

- Articles
- Off-site blogs
- Press releases
- Social networking profiles
- Social bookmarking profiles

Pay-per-click Results

Sponsored results, or pay-per-click results, are instant exposure for your business. They appear at the very top of results, as well as to the right of results. A carefully written ad can give great results in converting site visitors to customers. Be sure to make a budget for PPC ads and stick to it because it can get out of hand. It is the fastest way to get traffic to your site and is an important and valuable online marketing strategy.

Content Results

Online domination comes when your content is in the top results of a search for your keywords. For example, if someone searches for a given keyword that you have used in your online marketing strategy and among the top five results they get are your business website ranked number one, one of your videos ranked number four and one of your press releases ranked number five, chances are that searcher will recognize you as the online authority. This means the potential client is very likely to choose your business over another to meet its needs.

Getting this type of result is easy to do because Google loves content from Web 2.0 applications, like online articles, press releases and videos. If your content is out there and is presented in an SEO format, you will find that getting multiple places at the top of a search is the norm.

With the use of the 4-point online domination model, you will be able to get the outstanding results you are looking for.

Your Simple Online Marketing Plan

An online marketing plan is a must! In order to succeed you need to have a structured plan and work through it, knowing exactly what needs to be done. Below is a simple online marketing plan you can put in place for your business:

- Identify your ideal customers and what keywords they search with.
- Use personal branding to gain trust in the online marketplace.
- Optimize your website layout and use search engine optimization.
- Start the 4-point online domination (use local business results, natural search results, PPC results and content results).
- Get ranked in the local business results.
- Get in all the online business directories.
- Use all of the "local sites" to get tons of links which equals high natural search results.
- Utilize simple article marketing.
- Have a blog and consistently make posts using "long-tail" keywords to improve your ranking on the search engines.
- Create Internet videos and put them on your site and distribute on video sites.
- Create Internet audios and put them on your site and distribute on audio/podcast sites.

Big Fish Results

- Compose online press releases.

- Make use of PPC by using targeted "local" keywords and geo-targeting "generic" keywords.

- Monitor and optimize how much traffic is getting to your site, how many new customers are being converted from that traffic, how keywords ranked and what has been done to cause these changes.

- Apply social media and social networking techniques.

- Use local discussion forums.

- Use classified ad sites like Craigslist.

- Set up an autoresponder and build an email list for your business (get the power of "Customers and Cash on Demand!")

Prior to Putting Your Online Marketing Plan in Place

Before you begin putting your new online marketing plan in place, you should analyze what exactly you have done to date in terms of your website and online marketing and therefore what is most pressing. You cannot achieve everything at once, so by being thorough about it, you can effectively spot where best to begin. Evaluate your current status so you get a clear up-to-date picture of where you are starting from, where you want to go and what must be done to get there.

Analyze Your Overall Online Marketing Plan

Ask yourself the following questions about your current online marketing:

- How do you market your company?
- How do you promote your web presence already?
- Do you use pay-per-click ads?
- How much do you spend on those ads? Are they working?
- How many unique visitors does your site get per month?
- What type of training does your sales team undergo?
- Why do you want to put an online marketing plan in place?
- What is the value of your average sale?
- Are you capable of exponential growth?
- What percentage of your revenues comes from leads generated by the Internet?
- How many sales/leads do you get per month from your website?

Big Fish Results

- What traffic techniques do you currently use to drive traffic to your website?
- How much are you currently spending each month to get that traffic?
- What is the average revenue per sale?
- What is the average profit per sale?
- On average, how often does a customer buy from you?
- Approximately how many current customers do you have?
- Approximately how many customers have ever bought from you?
- Do you periodically touch base with them? If so, how often and how?

At the end of these questions, you should have a good report card on the overall health of your Internet marketing plan as it now is for your business. The answers to the above questions will let you know if it is working or not. It also starts to uncover some of the potential for growth that your business has!

Analyze Your Online Marketing Plan for Each Line

For each specific service or product you offer, ask the question:

- Do you target local business results on Google?
- Are you registered with the online local business directories?
- Do you use search engine optimization to show up for the natural search results?
- Do you use article marketing?

- Do you have a blog? If so, how often do you post?
- Do you have videos on your site?
- Do you use videos on YouTube and other locations to promote your site?
- Do you use online press releases?
- Do you use pay-per-click?
- Do you test and track your main web pages?
- Do you use online classified ad sites?
- Do you use online local forums?
- Do you use audio marketing on your site and also syndicate the audio on other popular sites?
- Do you use email list building on your website?

All of the above methods should be in place in order to effectively market your business through your website. In fact most of these things should be done for each of the different product lines or services you carry. This is especially true if you target different markets, like residential and commercial. You need different approaches to reach each one and while you may send them back to the same site, your pay-per-click campaign, landing pages, online classified ads, local forums, email lists, videos, audios, articles and blogs should be tailored to each market.

Where to Start

If you are looking at the overall job of setting an effective online marketing plan in place for your business, it seems rather daunting. However, if you look more closely at the list of online marketing tasks there are many things that will make a difference to your strategy and they are just one-time tasks. Start with them. Make sure you keep track of when they are completed to ensure you haven't missed something very important.

The one-time tasks that you must begin include:
- **Find your ideal customers.**
- **Do detailed keyword research.**
- **Do onsite search engine optimization updates.**
- **Add a lead capture system to your website.**
- **Do personal branding changes.**

Set yourself a deadline on the completion of these tasks. While these things are essential to increasing your online presence, if you just do them alone it will take a long time to rise through the search results, if at all. These tasks are the foundation of your marketing plan. Without them, many of your other strategies will fail, so they are very important to do and to do well. However, don't simply do these and then stop.

Doing Detailed Keyword Research

Hand-in-hand with the whole process of identifying your ideal customer is doing detailed keyword research. Even if you know who your ideal customers are but have no idea how to lead them to your site, you will not be successful in converting them to actual customers. This is typically a one-time task done at the beginning of your online marketing campaign and can be delegated to a keyword research specialist for extremely effective results.

The Necessity of Keyword Research

Keyword research is like turning on the light. By doing keyword research you will know, and not guess, exactly what your potential customers are searching for when they look for services and products like you offer. Simply knowing who your ideal customers are is not enough. You have to know the phrasing they use when they search. When you discover those phrases, your keyword research is done.

Luckily, the keyword research portion of the marketing plan only needs to be done once, unless you diversify the line of products or services you offer, new uses are discovered for them or you open a new division of your company.

In order to nail down the keywords that are being used to find companies in your field, ask yourself some questions.

How Will People Search for You?

What types of phrasing will potential customers use when searching for you? Will they look for a person, position, a firm or a solution? Will they use geographic modifiers like a city, state or region? Will their level of motivation come through in their search by using specific words? Here are various examples of the ways in which people conduct online searches to find what they're looking for:

- **Specific Person:**
  - Plumber
  - Plumbing contractor

- **Geographic Modifiers:**
  - Plumber Atlanta
  - Plumber Atlanta, GA

- **Motivation Levels:**
  - Emergency plumber Atlanta
  - 24 hour plumber

As a critical part of your keyword research, you should employ a keyword research tool. While there are a variety of such tools on the market, Google Keyword Tool (External) is a free one that can help greatly, as it generates keyword ideas for you, as well as synonyms. Cross-reference your keywords with geographic modifiers. This will often help you be as effective as possible in getting ranked according to strong keywords. The more precise the keyword, the better conversion rate it will have for sales.

Use **Market Samurai (http://www.MarketSamurai.com)** or another pay site for further building a list of long-tail keywords. They can help you determine which very specific keywords are most valuable. It will also give you an inside look into which words your competitors are using and the quality of the SEO competition they present, when you do a keyword search for them.

Document Data for Future Use

Be sure to keep a running tab of all the keywords you discover. This will give you information to work with for your online content. It will also keep you from having to repeat the keyword search.

Keywords will be used in every aspect of your online marketing. Therefore, the research you do in the beginning about your ideal customer and how they search will carry over in all your online content. You will use those keywords for:

- Articles
- Blogs
- Search engine optimization

- Press releases
- Ads
- Social media
- Videos and audios
- Tags

Even simply adding one or more traffic methods per month to your existing traffic generating strategies will produce significant results. Target a couple more keywords from your keyword list each month.

Do Onsite Search Engine Optimization Updates

This one-time activity will transform your website from whatever it is presently to a search engine optimized version that is much more attractive to web crawlers. This is extremely important in getting your website ranked as high as possible in the search engine results. The things that are appealing to a search engine are not the same as those things that are esthetically pleasing on a website. In many cases such fancy programming on a site is a negative for search engines.

Analyze What You Have

First you will need to begin by analyzing your current site, so look at these things:

- Consider the look and feel of the site.
- Is the site optimized for visitors?
- Is the site optimized for search engines?
- Does the site work for multiple browsers?

Critical Components of a Good Website

In most cases, websites are lacking in some of these areas. In order to make your website appealing to human visitors and search engines, and be effective in its purposes, you will need to go through and make sure certain things are in place. If they are not, you need to include the following for the best results possible:

- **Easy navigation:** Make sure the site is easy to use and straightforward.

- **Most important information "above the fold":** Make sure all the important information is visible when a visitor first arrives at the home page. A good number of people will not scroll down to find the important information.

- **All links correctly working:** Don't frustrate visitors or the search engines with broken links.

- **Home page, products page, services page, testimonials, about, and contact form.**

- **Directed navigation through the site:** Make sure you are taking visitors exactly where you want them to go on your site.

- **Specific instructions.**

- **Multiple calls to action:** Such as call now, buy now, etc.

- **Pictures used correctly:** This includes proper sizing of pictures as well as using captions to explain what the pictures represent.

- **Non-distracting design:** This goes for a background that is too distracting as well as crazy fonts, italics and underlines.

- **Centered layout that has dark text on a light background.**

- **Multiple ways to contact:** With the phone number on the top right, side and bottom, and the address only at the bottom.

- **Trust factors:** Like BBB and awards clearly displayed on the front page.

- **Testimonials on the front page.**

- **Personal branding:** This includes pictures of you and your staff, branded vehicles, audio and video messages and links to any social networking sites like Facebook or Twitter.

- **Optimization for keywords:** Using good keywords is huge for search engines and you must take some time to do keyword research before you can determine if keywords are optimized properly.

- **Relevancy:** Search engines love websites that show relevancy. This is done by starting broad and then drilling down in themes. Always optimize for one keyword per page instead of multiple keywords per page.

- **Ensure keywords are in all title tags, meta tags, the URL** and the headers and description of your pages.

- **Good content:** Guarantee all text on your website is search engine optimized with strategic use of keywords and avoid duplicate content.

- **Avoid Flash and frames.**

With the onsite SEO updates completed, your website should naturally move closer to the top of search engine results. However, you cannot rely on this alone. You must also continue with your online marketing plan and maintain a blog, do other Web 2.0 applications and submit articles with links back to your website in order to increase traffic and to get quality one-way links that will help you get to the very top of the results like you want and need.

Add a Lead Capture System to Your Website

By adding a lead capture system to your website you are taking the destiny of your business into your own hands. No longer are you simply a passive participant who casts a line and waits for the fish to come to you.

With a lead capture system you have the opportunity to get the names and contact information of people who visit your site for any reason. This means that you can now build a database of potential customers that you can market to. When you need more business you market to those people and you can create cash on demand.

All types of sales are dependent on leads. Therefore, having a lead capture system is a wise move in your online marketing strategy. It gives you something tangible to work from when you need more sales. And who doesn't need more sales?

Lead Capture Systems Defined

A lead capture system is simply an opt-in box that offers more information, an e-newsletter subscription, a free report or some other freebie in exchange for simple contact information. Typically the information requested is just a name and email address, but some systems do ask for a mailing address and/or a phone number. Try to refrain from requesting too much information.

Because these people have actually come to your site and then opted to get on your email list, you can feel confident that they are actually interested in your products or services. This makes them likely customers.

Once the lead capture system is in place on your website, you will need to do lead nurturing. This means you must stay in touch with these people. Here are some ways in which you can maintain contact:

- Send newsletters regularly, but not too frequently.
- Keep them up to date on new offerings and sales.
- Offer special deals for those on your email list. This is a very good way to generate business when things are slow.

As a part of this process you will need to do some of the things that were mentioned in the "Five Things No One Is Doing" section. You will need to put autoresponders in place, so that as people opt in, they are greeted, welcomed and introduced to your products or services through a series of letters. If you haven't used a free report to get them to join your email list, offer it now.

By building your email list and marketing to it regularly with useful information, you will get the power of having a bigger customer base and being able to generate cash on demand.

Building an Email List

There are a number of excellent reasons why you should start to build an email list for your business. Large companies recognize the value of email lists, but often small companies do not. However, you should know the many advantages of an email list:

- Multiple selling opportunities. If visitors come to your website and don't buy anything, once they leave, they may be gone for good. If however there is an email list for them to subscribe to then you will still be able to maintain contact with them and therefore have more chances to sell to that visitor.

- Send out special offers, holiday specials, breaking news, new product photos, and case studies, etc.
- More sales to existing customers. Because your existing customers will be on the email list they will also be in steady contact with you and this will allow you to give special offers and promotions that will induce further sales.
- More referral opportunities. You can utilize your email list to ask for and probably get more referrals.
- Creates a branding image.
- Positions you as an "expert" if done properly.

By effectively using your email list, you will be on your way to helping your business thrive. Smart businesses recognize the value of successful email lists and see growth in their sales.

Making Personal Branding Changes

By doing one-time personal branding changes, you can affect the kind of change you want in the results you get from your website. You want your website to have a certain kind of feel to it so you give the impression to visitors that you are indeed a trusted expert in your local market. By tapping into the unique resources the Internet offers, you can help do that and increase traffic and buying customers at the same time.

You are trying to appeal to a sophisticated audience. They are savvy to the things marketers throw at them. They research purchases much more than ever before. However, their attention spans are relatively short and they make decisions quickly. They are not completely at ease doing business online yet and question whether or not they should trust what they find there. When they come across your website they want to be sure it is the right source for what they are seeking. They want to know about your company, your commitment to service and your trustworthiness.

By putting the right content on your site you can build your personal brand and reassure your customers that you can offer what they are looking for. You want to personalize the process for new customers. They want to know about you and your business. Therefore, get personal and let them know who they are doing business with.

Stay away from the "stuffy" corporate sounding websites. No one wants to do business with a big company. They want to do business with neighbors they can trust. Some tweaks to your site can give that impression and help increase sales for you.

Some of the things to include on your website to help you create this personal touch include:

- Photographs and information about the owner and staff
- Expert articles you've written
- Reviews
- Awards
- Professional associations
- Business groups you are a member of
- References from other businesses
- Audio or video messages from the owner
- Audio or video testimonials from customers

You and your business need to be perceived as friendly, not stuffy. By taking the time to invest in personal branding, you will attract more and more buying customers. You will be gaining the trust needed to succeed in the online marketplace.

Tasks that Repeat

Once you have completed the one-time tasks for your local business online marketing plan, you will need to start on the tasks that repeat. These will need to become a regular part of your routine. While some of the repeated tasks are only done every month or even less often, others need to be done daily or a couple of times each week.

The tasks that you will need to do repeatedly in order to build-up your online presence and drive as much traffic as possible to your website include:

- Article marketing
- Press releases
- Video marketing
- Local SEO
- Natural SEO
- Pay-per-click campaigns
- Report generation
- Testing/tracking
- Blogging
- Directory submission
- Adding testimonials
- Web 2.0

Dealing with Tasks that Repeat

You can choose to take on these tasks yourself, delegate them to someone who works for you or subcontract them to a third party who specializes in such areas. If you hire a specialist, you can have them take on all of the above tasks or just select ones. Most subcontractors who specialize in online marketing give you an à la carte option or a package covering all your online marketing needs.

Scheduling the Tasks that Repeat

If you choose to do the online marketing tasks that repeat yourself, you will need to learn strategies for each and plan them into your work week. Regularity with such tasks is vitally important to the success of your marketing plan. Therefore, a good idea is to add your repeated tasks to your calendar/planner so they are done with the frequency that is necessary.

Article Marketing

Article marketing is simply the writing of approximately 500 word articles on a subject that is somehow related to your business or industry. These content-rich articles are then published online through a variety of article submission sites. The resource box, typically found at the bottom of the article, is how readers find your company information and are directed to your website. Article marketing is so simple that many people overlook its power and effectiveness.

The Importance of Article Marketing

Article marketing is one of the absolute best ways to put Internet marketing to work for your business. By strategically writing articles that are relevant to your industry and submitting them to online article submission sites you will create a direct path to your website for anyone who does a search for information that relates to your business.

Remember that an article is not a sales pitch. It needs to be full of relevant information that is actually useful and/or entertaining. It must also be written using search engine optimization techniques. Be careful not to keyword stuff your articles. Never plagiarize content from anywhere else.

Once you write good articles that actually teach your customers something while establishing yourself as a go-to expert in the industry you will need to get the articles published in a variety of places. EzineArticles.com and Squidoo.com are two excellent locations for publishing such articles, but ideally you will want to submit your articles to hundreds of websites. Article submission sites can help you do that. Be sure to avoid using duplicate content from your website as this may affect the ranking of your article and your site.

Articles are vital to your Internet marketing plan. Therefore, you will need to produce them regularly. This is where those seeking your keywords will stumble across your company, thanks to the resource box that is always included at the end of your articles. However, they actually have to get to the bottom of the page to get that information. That means you had better have a captivating article written to keep their attention!

Regular article publication will set you apart from many of your competitors, but you must be consistent. You must create multiple articles each month in order to keep traffic flowing to your site. Luckily, this is a very easy task to subcontract out.

Articles are meant to attract people to your site. They are published on other websites with backlinks to your site which creates an added bonus for you. As discussed before, the more backlinks there are to your site the better.

Use Articles to Create Interest and Reach All Potential Customers

To pique the interest of a wide variety of different possible customers, you will need to write a variety of articles, targeting a variety of subjects.

Big Fish Results

Make sure you write articles that touch on every use of your product or service. Some great article ideas are listed below:

- Tips on the use of your product
- Reasons why someone would want to use your service
- Unconventional uses for your product or service
- Frequently asked questions
- Individual products and services
- How to choose the best provider of your type of service or product
- Things to consider when purchasing
- The advantages of using your product or service
- The disadvantages of not using your product or service
- "How to" articles
- Things you shouldn't do
- Evaluations of different options
- Steps for using your products or services
- How your products or services help people
- Little known facts
- Explanations
- How to avoid a problem
- Tips on responding to a challenge

Once you have chosen a subject for an article, it should be in the 400-750 word range. Make sure it is well-written and flows naturally in order to keep people reading. Nothing turns a reader off faster than poor grammar and confusing sentences.

The simple formula for article writing as an online marketing technique is as follows:

- Do your keyword research.
- Get your content written.
- Submit it to article directories.

Press Releases

Online press releases are a huge part of building online traffic to your site. They are a credible way to build your online presence. Created to meet strict guidelines, they give select information in a standardized format. Press releases published on certain online press release distribution sites have the opportunity to be picked up and republished in other places. This greatly helps in the increase of traffic to your website through valuable backlinks.

You can create press releases for your business for a wide variety of reasons:

- The launch of a new product, service or line
- Hiring a new professional employee
- Creation of a new division
- Receiving an award
- Milestones in the life of a company
- Reorganization of a company
- Sales related to holidays
- Stock sales
- Partnerships

- Environmentally friendly steps the company is taking
- Contests
- Promotional programs
- New or improved website
- Expert opinions on subjects related to your industry
- Involvement in social causes
- Event involvement

Press releases build even more credibility for your company, as there are more stringent guidelines for the publication of press releases than there are for article publication. If your press release does not comply with the required format and content guidelines it will not get published. Therefore, many readers will take information shared in a press release even more seriously than articles or blogs.

Press releases will help get people talking about your business. It will also get you noticed by the search engines, so be sure to create a search engine optimized press release to increase its appeal to web crawlers. When you post it on sites that allow backlinks, press releases can also help direct traffic to your site. The call to action in your press release such as an offer of more information should always generate traffic.

Press releases need not be done as often as blogs or articles. However, you should strive to distribute at least one each month. This will set your business apart from the many competitors who do not do it.

Video Marketing

Video marketing is the hot thing in online marketing right now. It appeals to the kind of people who prefer watching videos to gain information rather than reading about it. In a culture that grew up on television, video marketing is an ideal way to get the message across. It can also be much more cost-effective than using TV advertising, which is too costly for the majority of local businesses, and is a much less-targeted form of marketing.

Video marketing offers a variety of creative options, including the option of teaching with slides of information being shown while a narrator speaks; pictures that give a great visual being presented to music or an actual video clip that has been produced. In fact you can even do a combination of these types.

Video marketing allows you to do the following:

- Give a tour of your facilities.
- Provide demonstrations.
- Instruct on the use of your products.
- Solve common problems.
- Provide amazing before and after samples for services.
- Present webinars.
- Share testimonials.
- Show company overviews.
- Share expert articles.
- Deal with questions.
- Present the company owner in an interview.

There are endless uses for video marketing. Because of the visual interest factor, it is useful both onsite and offsite to meet a variety of marketing needs:

- Use to grab the attention of visitors and have them "stick around" your site.
- Many lazy visitors would rather watch a short video than read a bunch of text.
- Use it to brand yourself.
- Use it to build trust.
- Use it to inform or educate visitors.
- Use it offsite to grab searchers and redirect them to your site or phone number.
- Use it to get rankings for multiple keywords or for rankings in suburbs of major metropolitan areas.
- Use it to spice up external landing pages and Web 2.0 properties.
- Get your business in multiple places.

Creating quality video is not a complicated process, but it does require time and some knowledge.

Mobile Marketing

The next wave of local marketing strategy your business needs to jump on is mobile marketing. Quickly becoming recognized as a mass media channel, marketing to your customers on their mobile devices is now one of the most powerful ways to reach them.

Mobile marketing's not a strategy you can just jump in and do, though. Just like any other form of advertising, if it's done poorly, you'll only succeed in irritating your prospective and current customers. If it's done well, you may be astounded by the results.

Currently, one reason mobile marketing is so effective is that the 'open rate' for text messages is nearly 100%. It would be nearly impossible to reach a success rate approaching anywhere near that figure with email marketing or direct mail.

Mobile marketing can effectively accomplish these tasks for your business:

- Increase brand awareness.
- Gather customer information for marketing purposes.
- Draw customers into buying mode more consistently.

Here are some mobile marketing tactics businesses are seeing success with now:

- Polls
- Trivia contests and sweepstakes
- Instant win games
- Free giveaways
- Alerts about sales and other deals
- Graphics and other messages that are so engaging they get forwarded to your customers' contacts

Mobile marketing strategies, like online marketing, are constantly evolving. If you begin a mobile marketing campaign, be sure that you learn, stay on top of, and follow the rules of the game so you don't inadvertently cause problems for your business.

Local SEO and Natural SEO

Search engine optimization, or SEO, is vital to the implementation of your online marketing plan. While this is a part of the five one-time things you must do to get your plan started successfully, it must also be monitored and updated, so that your local business results and your natural search results remain ranked near or at the top.

Local Business Results

Local business results will impact not only the traffic to your website, but also the phone at your place of business. Since your phone number is listed in the local business results you will find that your phone will ring much more often once your business is successfully located at the top of these results.

Submit your business to the three major local business results sites. Monitor and update listings regularly to secure top spots. Make sure that your listings are search engine optimized. **The three sites you <u>must</u> be on are:**

- **Google**
  - This is the most important one as it owns 2/3 of online traffic; your Google + Local Pages listing is especially vital to your success.
- **Yahoo**
  - This website is also very important.
- **MSN/Bing**
  - This one is growing in importance, but not as prominent as Google and Yahoo.

These local business results each pick up on select keywords and use different location modifiers when ranking listings. However, most listings include address, phone number, directions to your physical address, website and customer reviews. The ones with the best reviews containing targeted keywords, in addition to location modifiers will find their way to the top of the search results.

In order to be listed in the top 10 search results, **follow these seven tips**:

1. Optimize every aspect of your listing with strategic keywords.
2. Get reviews from customers.
3. Obtain backlinks from local online directories.
4. Strategically choose the areas you want optimized, even establishing different addresses and phone numbers for other areas.
5. Get listed in about four to five categories related to your business for your business results listing.
6. Place coupons with the listing to increase conversion rates.
7. Use YouTube Videos and photographs with your keyword in the title.

After listing in the top local business results, seek out other directory listings to use such as Kudzu, City Search, cmac.ws, Best of the Web local and more.

Track the changes you make, so that you can keep the listing as relevant and consistent as possible. It will also help you monitor what works and what doesn't. Be patient, it sometimes takes three to four weeks to see your listing appear.

Natural Results

Natural results are also referred to as organic results as they are generated by the search engines themselves and are not paid for.

Typically placed below local searches with the map and paid searches, many people consider them the most valid type of search results.

It is possible to get a variety of listings in the natural results. Anything that has relevant content on it, especially if it has been search engine optimized, can be included in natural results. Search engine rankings can include:

- Your main website
- Social media content
- Articles
- Press releases
- Other Web 2.0 content
- Landing pages
- Videos
- Social bookmarks
- Directory listings
- Blog posts

Keyword research is vital to the successful ranking of your website and other content in the natural results of search engines. Therefore this step is not to be overlooked. The relevancy of your content is very important to placement. Other ranking factors which impact where your content will show up in ranking results include:

- Content congruency/consistency
- Keywords used in page links
- Keywords in the content
- Backlinks
- Links pointing back to your site/content
- Google Page Rank

In fact, good relevant content with keywords and enough backlinks will be sure to make it to the top of many categories within a given period of time. Get links to your site from local directories, article marketing, Web 2.0, blogs, social bookmarks and video marketing. The more backlinks you have to your site, the more successful it will be in ranking.

Pay-per-click Campaigns

Pay-per-click campaigns are one area where many people are already investing in online marketing. You may be one of those who recognize the value of such campaigns in finding potential customers. One of the major advantages of PPC campaigns is the fact that you can be up and running with traffic actually coming to your website in as little as one day.

Pay-per-click campaigns can also be very expensive. However, they can be greatly downsized and often even completely eliminated by the effective use of an online marketing strategy. You can easily spend a lot less on your PPC campaigns than you have previously if your business is consistently at the top of search engine results. However, PPC campaigns are still important tools that can remain as a part of a good online marketing strategy, especially for extremely competitive keyword searches.

The Right Keyword Research

Keyword research will be the thing that makes your PPC campaigns work like never before. If you have your keyword research done correctly, you will have a list of keywords that are used when people search for something your business could provide, including very specific long-tail keywords. These keywords will not only be the ones most commonly used, but also the ones that have the fewest PPC matches for them. This means when someone uses those keywords your ad will appear at the top, not mixed in somewhere with endless others.

Keyword research makes all the difference between hit or miss PPC campaigns and ones that really work and have a high rate of conversions to sales for the number of click-throughs that you get. Having professional management of your PPC campaigns can mean huge savings and much greater results.

Geo-Targeting Your Ads

Most people are not familiar with this type of PPC option. However, it allows you to target your PPC ads to just the people in your area who are searching for a given term. Using geo-targeting, a search from someone in your geographic area for a generic term like "plumber" would reveal your ad, whereas someone in another state or area that you don't serve who searches for "plumber" would not see your ad.

Using Google Adwords and other PPC services you can choose to have your ads shown only to people living in certain zip codes, cities or regions. By doing so you can bid on very generic terms that previously would not have been a good choice. This is possible because search engines know where searchers are located. You can choose to target:

- Actual location
- Narrow geography such as city, state or metro area
- IP address

In addition you can choose to do PPC campaigns on words with a location qualifier attached to them. Many people will actually choose to include the location qualifier in their search, such as "Atlanta plumber." By using both the searcher's actual location and where the searcher is looking, you will have the greatest success possible in your pay-per-click campaign.

The advantages to geo-targeting generic terms for your PPC ads are:

- Cheaper click rates
- Fast traffic results

- More targeted traffic
- Lower competition
- Higher conversion to sales

The Importance of the Landing Page

A landing page is the page a prospect reaches when they click on your ad, on a link in your article's resource box, or on a link in a press release, video, or audio. The best-designed landing pages have a way these visitors can trade their contact information for a special report or some other content that's valuable to them. The landing page is a very important component in the online marketing strategy for pay-per-click campaigns. It should be relevant to the ad that you have placed and should contain keywords related to the search. You should have a different landing page for each PPC ad you place. Include navigation links to other parts of your website for even better results on Google.

Consider Using a Content Network PPC Campaign

Content network PPC allows you to sell advertising space on your own website and use space on other websites that relate to yours. What's most effective about advertising with the content network is the fact that most of the time people spend online isn't spent using a search engine, but visiting their favorite sites. Content PPC allows you to get your ad in front of them while they're on these popular sites.

A large number of websites collaborate in a content network and you get the advantage of the traffic attracted to each of them. Your ad can be so much more than a text ad like traditional PPC. You can opt for images and even video to capture the attention of potential customers. Content network PPC is wide open right now and is an excellent option to explore in your Internet marketing plan.

Report Generation, Testing and Tracking

Report generation must be done regularly in order to stay on top of the performance of your online marketing plan. Through testing and tracking you can effectively and clearly see what is working and what is not. **So then by doing more of what is working and less of what isn't working, you'll grow faster at less cost.** This is a very important part of your business and must be done at least quarterly, unless you are functioning beyond full capacity. As you are implementing, or even prior to implementing, your new marketing strategies take the time to test and track so that you have a baseline to compare against.

Use the following types of data in your analysis of your marketing:

- ▲ **Rankings**
- ▲ **Links/Backlinks**
- ▲ **Traffic Sources and Volume**
- ▲ **Visitor Data**
- ▲ **Visitor Actions and Behavior**

▲ **Rankings**
You will need to track the main site rankings for your different keywords. This will tell you where each keyword ranks, so you can get an idea of the ranking possibilities for the content you put out there using that keyword. You can use rank checking tools to assist you in tracking rankings for keywords. Check those of your competitors also.

▲ **Links/Backlinks**
When testing the backlinks of your site, you'll need to find out where links are coming from. This is also a test to make sure that links are actually working. Track how many backlinks your site has and how many are recognized by Google. Do the same for

your competitors, especially those who already have a good degree of online domination. This will give you ideas of where you need to link from. You can access link and backlink tracking tools to facilitate the process.

▲ **Traffic Sources and Volume**
Traffic sources and the volume of traffic need to be tracked and optimized. This will tell you where your visitors are coming from and the number of visitors you are getting from each source. It is important to know if they are direct visitors, referred through natural search engine results, referred from other sites or referred through paid search engine ads. This type of tracking will also reveal the keywords that are working to get visitors to your site. There are traffic tracking tools available for this.

▲ **Visitor Data**
Visitor data should also be tested, tracked and optimized as a regular part of your marketing program. You want to know where they are located, which web browser they use, the type of operating system they use, connection speed and if they are a brand-new visitor or a repeat one. This will help you create the best visitor experience possible for those who come to your site. The same tracking tools that provide traffic data will also help you track visitor data.

▲ **Visitor Actions and Behavior**
You will also need to track visitor actions and behavior information. Details like the page of the site the visitor entered on and exited from will divulge the relevant information they were looking for. With such information, you will learn how well your landing pages and other content are working for you. You can also find out how long they stayed on your site, which will help you come up with ways to keep them there longer.

Record the links that get the most click-through traffic, so that you know what information attracts visitors most. The most important feature of tracking visitor behavior is the fact that you can find out the number of people who took action and what they actually did. There are a variety of technologies that allow you to track such information.

By regularly testing and tracking your site with the collection of important data, you will be equipped to optimize it so you get the best results possible. You will know what is working well and what needs to be changed. Discern what the data actually means, so you can change content or make site adjustments if necessary. This will help you improve your business by getting the right people to your site who will then convert to sales.

Blogging

Blogging can be one of the most effective ways to get yourself to the top of the search engine results for your chosen keywords. Google and other search engines regularly visit blogs and re-index the content found there because they love such applications. Therefore, if you regularly blog, your site will get increasingly better results on search engines. As more and more backlinks are built, the traffic to your site will increase.

Shorter than an article with fewer guidelines than a press release, blogs can be quick and easy to produce. However, they must also meet SEO criteria for maximum effectiveness. This means you should focus on keywords, specifically long-tail keywords, when you blog. However, be sure to not stuff keywords into the text. It should have a natural flow so people keep coming back to it, actually want to read it and subscribe to your RSS feed.

Below are some tips for blogging:

- Keep blog posts short — under 400 words.
- Use keywords in the title and throughout the blog.
- Add an image for visual interest.

- Schedule the appearance of a new blog about every three days or even more often depending on the industry you are in.
- Make blogs relevant to what is happening in the news.
- Don't use a blog to rant about something. Keep it informative.

You can also use offsite blogs to increase traffic to your website by using Web 2.0 and offsite blogs such as:

- **Squidoo.com**
- **HubPages.com**
- **Xanga.com**
- **Vox.com**
- **Blogger.com**
- **360.Yahoo.com**
- **WordPress.com**
- **LiveJournal.com**
- **Zimbio.com**
- **Spaces.Live.com**

Create even more backlinks by submitting your offsite blog posts to social networking and social news sharing sites.

The Importance of Blog Comments

Your blog is essentially a forum whereby others will have the opportunity to interact with you. Those who make comments are likely to be potential customers or even existing customers. Always respond to valid questions, comments and complaints. The way in which you handle such things will speak volumes to the followers of your blog.

Bear in mind that you can learn a lot from the comments your blog receives. Your next big product or service is often waiting to be discovered in the feedback of a customer or potential customer. They may share with you what little thing bothers them most or what would be an ideal addition to what you offer. This interaction which allows you to garner knowledge from those who buy from you is one of the most important aspects of a blog. Use it!

You should also take the time to comment on other blogs related to your field and leave your own website address to create more valuable backlinks. Do not make a comment that is little more than an ad for your own business. It will likely not even be approved if you attempt to do so. Make relevant, helpful comments. Leave your website URL in the space provided only.

Directory Submission

Links are the key to getting listed high in search engine results. One-way links are what you want, so make sure you focus on getting your site listed in as many places as possible. Directory submissions are excellent ways to get your site's link out there, even though many people will tell you that business directories are outdated. They do indeed have great value in getting backlinks to your website.

The types of directories you should submit to include:

- Major directories, like the fee-based Yahoo directory and the free human-reviewed DMOZ
- Local directories, like local.com, localize.com, hotfrog.com and specific group directories like your local chamber of commerce
- Industry specific and niche directories, such as cmac.ws and other niche groups found through online searches

- Yellow Pages/411 directories like YellowPages.com, Superpages.com, Yellowbook.com, InfoUSA.com and Localeze.com
- Review directories like Kudzu.com, Insiderpages.com, Tripadvisor.com, AngiesList.com, BBB.org and Citysearch.com

These directories will help customers and potential customers locate your business much easier. Your business will typically be at or near the top of search results for a business name or the niche and location. Therefore, your presence in the relevant directories will get you near the top of results. Your website traffic and your phone inquiries will increase as a result of being listed in directories. For that reason, directory submissions are a solid part of any marketing plan.

Inclusion in directories will also validate a company's existence for search engines. It creates backlinks to the website and citations that help the search engines index a company. Newer directories with Web 2.0 capabilities even have the interactive option of adding reviews, which creates even more content for a site. This means better natural search results and local search results for your business.

Most directories are free of charge; however some have a fee associated with them. If it is a big-name, powerful directory, it may be worth the investment.

Review directories serve a variety of purposes, such as:
- Backlinks
- Citations
- Reviews
- Local rankings
- Building customer trust

Citations are becoming one of the most important reasons to make sure your business is included in review directories. Essentially a citation is a third-party endorsement of your business. It acts as a vote of confidence Google can lean on in including your business at the top of Google + Local Pages results. Citations create credibility for your site in the eyes of the search engines. The more citations your business has, linking from other reputable sites, the better.

Adding Testimonials Creates Validity and More

Testimonials are an excellent way to build consumer confidence in your products or services. Visitors to your site witness actual customers and their level of satisfaction with your company. They see how your products are put to use and also get ideas as to how they can use them.

You can add video testimonials for maximum impact, as they appeal to everyone, even those who typically don't take time to read websites, and create a type of social proof that helps your personal branding. Alternatively you can post a testimonial in text form with accompanying pictures of the client and even the client using your company's services or products. You can also use simple audio clips for testimonials.

Some tips for the use of testimonials:

- Get testimonials from both genders.
- If your product or service is used in a variety of different ways or industries, get testimonials from various areas.
- Put some diversity of age and ethnicity in your testimonials.
- Feel free to use just a portion of a testimonial if it is too lengthy.
- Ask customers for testimonials that you can use.

New customers feel more confident about their decision to purchase from you if you have testimonials on your site. They get the impression that they are a part of a group and are not just another sale.

In every testimonial you must include:

- Customer's name and title
- City and state
- Credentials

Encourage them to talk about the way your business helped to solve their problem. Always get permission from the person to use the testimonial and information in it before publishing it. Keep a copy of the permission for reference.

The Importance of Web 2.0

Web 2.0 is a term used to refer to any applications that allow users to interact. Social networks, blogs, video sharing sites, wikis and more are some of the commonly used Web 2.0 applications that can be used as an effective part of any online marketing campaign. In fact, many of these types of applications allow an excellent source for feedback to a company.

One of the major purposes of using Web 2.0 in your quest to drive traffic to your website is to create backlinks to your site. So you will need to make comments on other sites with links back to your own sites. You will also need to create your own blogs, videos and social network identities to share useful information for those who would be potential customers for you.

As with any of the online writing you do, pay close attention to make sure that it is search engine optimized. Use keywords strategically in your content. This will ensure that you get the best ranking possible in relevant searches.

By using Web 2.0, you are opening up your business to explosive growth. It is easy for fans of your service to share it with others.

The feedback you receive from Web 2.0 gives you a wealth of opportunities:

- As individuals leave testimonials, you build credibility.
- As customers leave comments and suggestions, you get important feedback that allows you to tweak your product to best serve your customers. You will be much more on target with their needs.
- As complaints are dealt with your reputation for customer service is built.

Right now, Google, the leading search engine worldwide, loves Web 2.0 content such as:

- Videos
- Press releases
- Articles

Therefore, careful use of search engine optimized content on such sites will help give you the ranking you want on the search engines.

Social Media and Social Networking

Web 2.0 applications must be updated very regularly. Among your arsenal of tools in this category should definitely be Facebook, LinkedIn and Twitter. These are very important online marketing tools for most businesses which have a strong online presence. However, they must be updated regularly, preferably daily. This makes it a very daunting task for anyone who is short on time or is not a fan of social networking.

Think of Facebook as an extension of your email list. More and more people are shying away from communicating through email and are instead using Facebook. You can create an account that lets customers and potential customers friend you.

As you build your network of friends, be sure to regularly post specials, information about products and services and more. Status updates should be used to share brief tidbits of information similar to an abbreviated version of a newsletter or a special announcement that you would make through your email list. As friends interact with you and leave comments be sure to answer their messages. This will help you develop a relationship, which is becoming more and more important to people in their choice of who they do business with.

You should also take the time to "friend" other businesses that are complimentary to yours. A comment you make on a status they put up could be seen by countless potential new customers.

Twitter is like a mini-Facebook with only short Tweets allowed instead of long-winded status updates. You can follow others who Tweet and build a following of your own. Twitter is instantaneous and reaction to anything you put there can be very fast.

Among the social media sites that you should be familiar with are:
- Facebook
- Twitter
- YouTube
- LinkedIn
- Google Profiles
- Social bookmarking sites

Additional Traffic Strategies

By using a wide variety of traffic strategies, you will have the best chance of being able to attract the maximum number of potential customers to your website. Apart from the techniques already mentioned, there are other ones that will help you drive traffic to your site. Some of them are even completely free, while others involve a varying amount of investment depending on the quality of equipment you want to use to create the medium.

Classified Ads

By placing carefully created online classified ads you can easily drive traffic to your website. Many of these websites are free of charge, like Craigslist.org. You can choose to put an ad in the sections that best fit the services or products your company provides. You can even put links directly back to your website in many of these ads. The sheer volume of traffic on such sites will help people find you and your website more readily, as there are numerous people who use such sites as their go-to resource for many things.

To get the maximum amount of use from your classified ads, create links to your ad using social bookmarking sites and other social networking sites. This will create additional backlinks to your ad and help it get ranked on the search engines. Any content that gets ranked on the search engines is excellent for your online marketing.

Make sure the ads you place on classified ad sites are search engine friendly, like all your online content. Use keywords correctly, without stuffing them into the ad, to maximize your search engine result ranking. Such ads need to be placed monthly to stay current on the search engines. Vary the content though and add seasonal specials, if appropriate.

Some of the best classified ads sites include:

- Craigslist.org
- Backpage.com
- Topics.com/classifieds/city
- Olx.com
- Oodle.com
- UsFreeAds.com

Local Online Discussion Forums

Make sure you are active in local online discussion forums, as this will help you reach even more potential new customers. Many times people seek out such forums in an attempt to solve a problem they are facing. By being present and taking part in the discussions, you can offer your services to solve appropriate issues. In addition, you will be connecting with potential customers who speak openly about what they can't find or are not being offered. It is a great way to do research in order to fine-tune your offerings to make sure you are actually meeting the needs of those you want to buy from you.

You can find such local forums by doing a simple online search for them. Most require you to create a free account and profile that should include information on your business including a link to your site.

Some tips for optimal use of local online discussion forums as a part of your marketing strategy include:

- Start or contribute to conversations in a relevant way.
- Pay close attention to the forum rules.
- Realize that blatant advertising is a no-no.

- Use an anchor text keyword in your signature.
- Use "how to" articles as good posting content for the forums.

Post weekly or monthly on local online discussion forums to take advantage of the benefits, such as multiple backlinks, that are generated from each post.

Audio Marketing

By doing audio marketing you can more easily capture the attention of visitors to a site and get them involved in the content you are delivering. In fact, every business owner should incorporate audio marketing both onsite and offsite into their marketing plan. It is much more memorable than text and keeps visitors on a website longer than they would stay otherwise, because audio is more of a personable approach.

You can use audio to:

- Introduce your products or services
- Present the owner of the business
- Give consumer tips
- Give instructions
- Present testimonials
- Repurpose radio commercials
- Read blog posts or expert articles
- Give a call to action

In fact audio testimonials are a much more effective way of building trust with potential customers.

Offsite audio can be used to drive traffic to your website and to help with the personal branding of your business. It helps the owner appear to be a true expert in the field. Offsite audio also provides backlinks to your site and counts as content to help your site's ranking on the search engines.

Opt to put offsite audio on podcasts, online radio shows or other forms of distribution. You might also want to record a message with expert tips and link it back to your site, to promote yourself as an expert.

Create a title starting with your chosen keyword phrase when you submit your audio to different sites. Use the same keyword in the segment description. You can also drive traffic to your audio content with backlinks using various online marketing techniques. There are many tools that will help you facilitate the use of audio in your online marketing.

Keeping on Top of Things

By keeping a finger on the pulse of your industry you will easily find new topics for blogging, articles, press releases, videos, audios and even social networking comments. This way you can quickly jump on new trends as they become popular. Technology can help you do so by staying on top of the latest developments, trends and hot spots in online marketing. You will have a much better chance to keep your online market domination. There are always new developments in the dynamic world of online marketing. Therefore, staying abreast of new technologies and new trends is essential. You can do so by:

- Seminars
- Webinars
- Following blogs
- Watching the competition
- Subscribing to RSS feeds
- Being on email lists
- Social media

In addition you can use Google Alerts to stay on top of things happening in the media in either your industry, in a field relevant to yours, as well as in online marketing trends. By setting up a Google Alert, you are automatically informed when information concerning the topics you choose is updated in selected online formats. This helps you to keep on top of things so that you can share relevant information in a timely manner and drive people to your website for relevant solutions.

Outsourcing:
The Answer to Easy Implementation

Online marketing, like any marketing, is multi-faceted and requires a great amount of work and a hefty learning curve for those who have never done it before. Today's marketing requires a lot more maintenance than previously. Even just monitoring your Web 2.0 applications that should be checked daily can eat up precious time in your schedule.

It's All about Time

By outsourcing your online local marketing, you can ensure that your online marketing is done by those who are skilled in the field. You can conserve your own time to spend on the tasks in your company that rely on you. In addition the implementation of your marketing changes that are necessary to affect a change in your sales will get done much quicker than if you had to learn how to do it and then do it yourself.

Most business owners are spending 80+ hours weekly in their business, doing the things that are necessary to be successful. These people are masters of their domains and know what they are doing in their field of expertise. However, taking extraordinary amounts of time to learn and master Internet marketing does not always make sense. What does make sense is for them to continue doing the things they know how to do well and let a master in Internet marketing take care of that side of things for them. That is time and resources well spent.

Time is a crucial factor when you think about marketing your business. With the help of a professional Internet marketer, your business could easily rank number one in Google searches for local keywords in only one week. If you were to do it yourself, where would you be in the process of implementing your online marketing plan? Would you still be learning, procrastinating or would you actually have things done? Do you have the time to devote to this?

Internet marketers can take care of things such as:

- ▲ Site design
- ▲ Landing pages for PPC campaigns
- ▲ Video creation (slide show style)
- ▲ Video marketing
- ▲ Article marketing
- ▲ Directory submissions
- ▲ SEO
- ▲ Backlink generation
- ▲ PPC campaign management
- ▲ Social networking setup
- ▲ Email marketing setup
- ▲ General marketing consulting

In each of these categories there are so many more tasks that must be mastered before implementing them effectively on your website. By hiring a professional, all aspects can be taken care of quickly and easily.

▲ **Site Design:**
This can be much more than just creating a site from scratch. Internet marketers can also do any of the following:

- Site cleanup
- Meta tag cleanup
- Total redesign
- Set up contact forms
- Add audio
- Add video

▲ **Landing Pages for PPC:**
Internet marketers can help you set up a landing page that:
- Has proper keyword density
- Has an opt-in or capture page for collecting emails to be used later

▲ **Content Creation:**
There is a wide range of services an Internet marketer can handle:
- Website content
- Blog writing
- Article writing
- Email messages
- Free giveaway reports
- Capture page writing
- Press release writing

▲ **Video Creation:**
This can be done in the form of slide show or even live action. Here they can create videos for:
- Your website
- Capture pages
- Offsite properties
- Video marketing

▲ **Video Marketing:**
Just what it sounds like, this is marketing with video. This can be done by:
- Submitting to video sharing sites
- Repurposing for multiple keywords and submitting to other sites
- Submitting to external blogs

▲ **Article Writing:**
Some Internet marketers and article writing services can:
- Ghostwrite your articles for publication
- Write to submit to article directories
- Position for branding and backlinks

▲ **Directory Submissions:**
This is key for any business and can be done by:
- Submitting to top directories
- Submitting to local directories
- Submitting to niche directories
- Picking a number of directories they will submit your site to each month

▲ **SEO and Backlink Generation:**
Get your website ranked higher in the search engines by:
- Onsite optimization
- Backlinks galore
- Pick the number of backlinks you want them to add every month

▲ **PPC Campaign Management:**
They manage your PPC campaigns with:
- Google AdWords
- Yahoo Sponsored Search
- Microsoft Ad Center
- Lesser known PPC spots

▲ **Social Networking Setup:**
This is becoming more and more popular these days and with this they can:

- Set up profiles on Twitter, LinkedIn and Facebook
- Tweak backgrounds
- Add content
- Create groups
- Add friends/followers

▲ **Email Marketing Setup:**
Internet marketers can help you capture emails and use those emails to market:

- Send giveaway reports
- Set up capture pages
- Set up an autoresponder
- Write a series of emails

▲ **General Marketing Consultant:**
The sky's the limit here and Internet marketers can provide:

- Anything that will improve your business
- Guidance and instructions on setting up any of the other business tactics from above

In addition to any or all of these tasks, an Internet marketer can become your online marketing partner, doing all your Internet marketing tasks for you on a constant basis. This makes you essentially competition proof, because there is someone staying on top of it all for you and constantly getting more and more links and ranking you for more and more keywords.

Choosing the Right Subcontractor

If you decide that subcontracting your online marketing out to another firm is the right decision for you, take the time to find the right subcontractor. You should begin by deciding what you want done and what you plan to do yourself. It is fine to let a subcontractor do it all.

Next find an online marketer who is an authority in the field. Good choices are those individuals who make presentations for business groups on the topic of Internet marketing. Other good choices are those who appear at the top of natural local searches for Internet marketers because that means they can actually do what they say they can do. If an online marketer is everywhere, including in the top several spots in searches, you can feel confident that they are a leader in the field and a good choice for you.

Options in Outsourcing

There are so many different Internet marketers who offer some or all of the things above. Some specialize in just one area, while others offer all online marketing services. You need to determine if you want to take care of any of the tasks yourself, with an employee or through a professional. Internet marketers will often provide a variety of options for you to choose from to tailor the service you are purchasing to your needs.

- ▲ **A La Carte:**
  This is ideal for those who want to keep a hand on things and have a good knowledge of some of the areas of Internet marketing. It also works well for those who want to learn some of the specialties mentioned here.

- ▲ **Package Deals:**
  The perfect solution for the busy local business person who does not have the time or interest in learning the details of Internet

Big Fish Results

marketing. It allows for quicker implementation of all the different parts of Internet marketing as there is no learning curve involved. Those who will be doing your marketing already know what they are doing. You just need to prepare for the influx of new business.

▲ **Purchasing Leads:**
There are companies out there who have done all the Internet marketing in your domain and have the Web 2.0 applications in place. They have gathered leads for the type of products and services you deal in. You can simply purchase leads from such companies and follow up on them yourself.

▲ **Continuity Programs:**
With the purchase of a continuity program, you have an Internet marketer on retainer. These individuals offer programs whereby they implement new marketing strategies monthly over a fixed period of time or they do all the implementation of the strategies at the beginning and simply maintain them over a given period of time.

Online Marketing for Local Business Conclusion

Your online marketing strategy is based on getting more potential customers to your site and converting them into paying customers. It really is that simple. Through using a wide variety of techniques you can pinpoint those customers and make sure they find your business when they search online for products or services that you provide. When they find your website, a variety of other online marketing tools will be waiting to convert them into buying customers.

In order to do this effectively, most of your focus will be on two major aspects of your marketing plan: using keywords in all online content and creating as many links as possible to your website. The more backlinks you have, the better your site will place in search engine results and the more people will find your website. The more effectively you use keywords, the more search engine friendly your content is and therefore more likely to be ranked.

The more visitors you get to your website, the better your chances will be to get more new customers. New customers mean an increase in sales and profit as previously mentioned when reviewing the potential for exponential growth with online marketing for your business.

Techniques to Increase Your Business's Profits

Whether you have suffered a downturn in your business, have never built it to the level you are aiming for or if you are just starting out, your goal needs to be using online marketing strategies to increase your profits. **There are <u>four basic ways</u> to improve profits:**

1. **Increase customers**
    a. Increase traffic to increase customers.
    b. Add to product offerings to make them more compelling.
    c. Use PPC, SEO, local business results, article marketing, etc.

2. **Increase number of transactions per customer**
    a. Build a mailing list.
    b. Increase customer communications through autoresponders, newsletters and broadcast messages.
    c. Offer them upsell opportunities — pitch something seasonal.
    d. Send out reminders for services and specials.

3. **Increase the average dollar amount per transaction**
    a. Offer bundle packages and upgrades and stronger reasons to purchase.

4. **Decrease costs, finding free traffic, lowering cost per click**
    a. Increasing conversions thereby decreasing costs.
    b. Offer a bonus, change a headline or offer a free consultation.
    c. Even converting from 1% to 2% is a 100% improvement and cuts costs for buying traffic in half — pure profit!

By putting an online marketing plan in place and following through with it, you can achieve all of these goals. You can easily improve your profits through the strategic use of online marketing techniques that will increase customers, increase the number of transactions per customer, increase the average dollar amount per transaction and decrease costs while finding free traffic which leads to a lower cost per click.

Take the time today to investigate if your website is doing all it can to attract new customers for you. If not, get started putting the simple online marketing plan into place on your own or with the help of a professional.

Get started now on your online marketing plan to rescue your business. *Good luck!*

Made in the USA
Charleston, SC
19 August 2013